BECOME UNFORGETTABLE

BECOME UNFORGETTABLE

Sumit Kkhubchandani

Available on amazonkindle

Worldwide Published by

Pendown Press

PREMIUM BUSINESS PUBLISHER

PENDOWN PRESS LLP

An ISO 9001 & ISO 14001 Certified Co.,

Regd. Office: 3767A, Kanhaiya Nagar,

Tri Nagar, Delhi-110035

Ph.: 8130886000, 9650072927

E-mail: info@pendownpress.com

Branch Office: 1A/2A, 20, Hari Sadan, Ansari Road,

Daryaganj, New Delhi-110002

Ph.: 011-45794768

Website: PendownPress.com

Edition: 2025

Price: ₹ 499

ISBN: 978-93-7217-620-9

Layout and Cover Designed by Pendown Graphics Team

Dedication

To the capable who stayed quiet and paid the price for it.

To those who built value before visibility and wondered why recognition lagged behind.

To my parents, for teaching me responsibility, resilience, and faith long before the world taught me voice.

To my team members, who carried the weight of this journey with me.

This book is not mine alone.

It belongs to everyone, ready to be seen for who they are, not just what they've built.

TABLE OF CONTENTS

A Note From The Heart

It's funny...

People think you write a book alone. But the truth is, this one was written with hundreds of hearts beating beside mine.

To my father, Mr. Dalip Khubchandani, who taught me that true strength lies not in never falling, but in rising every time we fall, thank you for showing me how to lead with grit and grace.

To my mother, Mrs. Vineeta Khubchandani, whose prayers have been the invisible thread weaving through every success, your faith in me has been my compass.

To my team members- past and present, you are the unsung heroes of this journey.

To my mentors and coaches, who saw potential in me long before I did - your wisdom turned my stumbles into stepping stones.

Akshar Sir, you have been nothing less than an angel in my life. I say this without hesitation and with complete surrender of my heart that you gave birth to Sumit 2.0. You scolded me when I needed direction, you held up a mirror when I needed truth, and you taught me life all over again when I thought I already knew it. You helped me discover my why, my purpose, and most importantly, you made me see and value the talent that was always within me but waiting to be believed in. Your confidence became my wings. When you said, "I am your papa," something shifted inside me forever. This son carries that line with pride and responsibility. I promise you this from my heart and soul, I will make you shine, I will honour your faith, and I will make this papa feel proud

Tony Robbins

Tony taught me that in one decision, you can change the direction of your entire life.

Dan Lok

Dan taught me that money doesn't follow hard work; it follows value and positioning.

Robin Sharma

Robin taught me that true success begins with mastering the self, not the spotlight.

Paritosh Pathak

Paritosh taught me that your biggest breakthroughs happen when you stop running from yourself and the power of networking.

Ali Abdaal

Ali taught me how to use YouTube and that productivity is not hustle, it is alignment, clarity, and joy.

Rahul Jain

Made me a person who understands the power of lifelong learning, manifesting life, and managing operations.

T. Harv Eker

Harv taught me that until you change your money blueprint, no amount of effort will ever change your results.

To my Wife, Inayaa, and children Jahaan and Neihaan, and **my sister Kaira,** my anchors in life's stormiest seas, your love is my forever fuel. You waited through 18-hour days, missed vacations, and endured unheard apologies. But more than that, you gave me permission to dream.

To **Mr. Krishan Kumar Yadav** and **Mr. Aman Jain,** who are the main pillars of my Journey. **To my amazing publisher, Dinesh Verma, CEO of Pendown Press,** and his wonderful team, for making the book-writing and publishing process smooth, hassle-free, and enjoyable with their professional support and guidance. **And to friends, family, and my extended tribe,** your laughter, criticism, and unwavering support sculpted the entrepreneur, author, and human I am today.

Dil se *shukriya.*

This book, this journey, this life, is your masterpiece, not mine.

Love

Sumit Kkhubchandani

WHY THIS BOOK?

"Your brand is what other people say about you when you're not in the room."
~ Jeff Bezos

I didn't wake up one day and decide to write a book.

This book happened because I kept seeing the same pattern, again and again.

Good people.

- Capable people.
- People who had done the hard work.

And yet, somehow, they were still unseen.

I met business owners who knew every detail of their product but struggled to explain their own value.

- Founders who had built solid companies but were still introduced as "someone's son" or "the person behind the scenes."
- Professionals who delivered exceptional results, only to watch louder, less capable people win the room.

For years, I thought this was just how business worked.

- That recognition comes slowly.
- That visibility is optional.
- That humility means staying quiet.

Then I realised something uncomfortable.

- Silence isn't humility.
- Silence is expensive.
- I've lived that silence myself.

The silence of doing everything right, yet feeling overlooked. The silence of building something meaningful, but not being known for it. The silence of carrying responsibility early and postponing your own voice.

This book exists because that silence costs more than most people realise.

- It costs opportunities.
- It costs confidence.
- It costs growth.
- And slowly, it costs belief.

This is not a book about becoming famous.

It's not about social media tricks or personal branding jargon. It's not about changing who you are.

It's about making sure the world can finally see the person who's already doing the work.

- I wrote this book for the ones who stayed in the background too long.
- For the ones who believed their work would speak for itself.
- For the ones who kept waiting for the "right time" to step forward.

If you've ever felt that gap between what you've built and how you're seen,

This book is for you.

Not to make you louder.

But to make you visible.

BECOME UNFORGETTABLE

Because you didn't build all this just to remain invisible.

And because the world doesn't just need what you do. It needs to know who you are.

Before you turn the page, hear it in their voice.

Scan to watch how people like you moved from being overlooked to being seen.

SETTING CONTEXT

Before you begin, let me share something honest with you.

This isn't a book I decided to write. This is a book that grew inside me, page by page, through twenty years of watching brilliant people disappear.

- I've stood on factory floors where owners knew every machine's hum but couldn't recognize their own voice.
- I've sat in boardrooms where founders could explain complex financial models but couldn't articulate their own worth.
- I've watched legacy businesses pass from one generation to the next, carrying everything except the founder's story.

And I've felt it myself.

- ➔ The strange silence that comes when you've built something significant, but the world still introduces you as someone's son.
- ➔ The quiet frustration of delivering exceptional value, only to watch clients choose a louder, less capable competitor.
- ➔ The hollow feeling of building an empire that bears your family name, but never truly carries your soul.

This book was born in that gap, between what you've built and how you're seen.

It wasn't created in a consulting room or a content studio. It was written in hospital corridors while my father fought cancer, in market stalls where dreams get traded for practicality, in late-night realizations that the most important work I'd ever do wasn't building products—it was building people.

Personal branding isn't what you think it is.

- It's not shouting on social media.
- It's not pretending to be someone you're not.
- It's not chasing followers or likes or vanity metrics.
- It's something much quieter, and much more powerful.

It's the courage to finally stand in your own light.

- ➔ To let your work be seen.
- ➔ To let your story be heard.
- ➔ To let your value be recognized.

This book is my hand reaching out to you, the capable, the talented, the quietly exceptional, saying:

"Enough hiding.

The world needs what you have.

But first, it needs to see who you are."

If you've ever felt undervalued…

If you've ever lost a deal to someone less qualified but more visible…

If you've ever looked in the mirror and wondered why your external success doesn't match your internal worth…

Then this book isn't just for you.

It's about you.

It's about reclaiming your narrative.

It's about building the one thing nobody can take from you: your undeniable presence. It's about entering rooms before you walk through doors.

It's about becoming the leader people follow, not because they have to, but because they want to.

You've spent years building everything around you.

Now, let's build the most important thing:

Your visible, authentic, powerful self.

If any part of this felt familiar, you can write to me.

sumit@iconicedge.org

INTRODUCTION
WHERE YOUR STORY BEGINS BEFORE THE WORLD KNOWS YOUR NAME

There is a moment.

It comes for every business owner. Every founder. Every person who has ever created something from nothing. The world outside is loud markets churn, competitors shout, customers demand, trends flicker and die on a screen.

And yet, inside you, there is a silence.

You've done everything right. You have built what others dream of, a company, a legacy, a high-income practice, a reputation in your circle. The foundations are solid. The work is good. Damn good.

And yet.

Somehow, the world doesn't see you. Not the real you. Not the you who lay awake sketching visions, who fought through the chaos of launch, who knows every hidden strength of what you've made.

If you've ever felt this, this quiet gap between your worth and your visibility. Let me tell you something: **You are not alone. I have stood in that exact silence.**

- Before I became "India's Personal Branding Guy"...
- Before Jack Martin became a name in millions of homes...
- Before Iconic Edge was even a thought...
- Before I helped a single business owner step into their authority...

I was an 18-year-old boy, standing lost in the roaring heart of Lajpat Rai Market.

Asia's biggest electronics bazaar is not a place. It's a sensory storm. A chaos of wires, shouts, haggling, sweat, ambition, and dust. The air itself hummed with deal-making.

In my pocket, I had an admission letter to study abroad. A ticket. A suitcase packed with a future I could almost touch.

Then, life intervened. My father fractured his leg. Recovery would take months. The family business needed a son. He needed a son.

In one conversation, a future vanished. I didn't get on that plane. Instead, I stepped into the market. Into the family ledger. Into adulthood.

Overnight.

From that day, I lived two parallel lives:

➔ The life I had.

➔ And the life I still wanted.

For years, I moved through the noise, the clang of our factories in Noida, Haridwar, Roorkee; the pressure of scaling Jack Martin; the weight of teams, products, P&L sheets. Through struggle, rise, fall, and rise again.

And always, underneath the noise of business, that same quiet question pulsed:

"Who am I becoming out here? And does the world even know I exist?"

Here is the truth no one tells you early enough:

- You can build companies.
- You can build factories.
- You can build wealth.
- You can build a portfolio that impresses your family.

But if the world doesn't know you, you are only ever known locally. Never globally. You are a well-kept secret, and in business, secrecy is a prison.

I watched for years as people bought brands and forgot the people behind them.

Then, Wharton happened. My master's degree.

- ➔ For the first time, I saw visibility engineered.
- ➔ I understood the calculated power of presence.
- ➔ The art of being known before you speak, trusted before you sell.

But life had one more lesson to teach me.

In 2017, my father was diagnosed with pancreatic cancer.

Once again, I stepped back. The factories, the legacy, the weight of it all back on my shoulders. My dreams, my own voice, were shelved. There was no time to pursue what I loved. No time to pursue who I was.

Those two years didn't just change me. They stripped me down to the raw nerve of my being and rebuilt me from the ground up.

And then… as if the universe decided the timing was finally, painfully perfect… **a magician walked into my life. AY.**

A mentor who didn't teach. He unlocked.

He asked questions I had buried:

- ➢ "What is your inner calling?"
- ➢ "What do you truly want?"
- ➢ "Who do you want to become when no one is watching?"

The clarity was instant, like a fog lifting.

➔ I wasn't meant to just build products.

➔ I wasn't meant to just sell electronics.

➔ I wasn't meant to stay behind the scenes.

I was meant to build people.

To build the stories, the authority, and the undeniable presence of those who create real value in this world. My mission became to show every talented, invisible business owner the one glaring gap in their legacy:

You have built everything.

Except yourself.

Iconic Edge was born from that truth.

And with it, lives began to change. A pattern emerged, again and again:

Brilliant minds, invisible.

Genius, undervalued.

Expertise, underpaid.

Leadership, undiscovered.

Not because of a lack of capability.

But because of a lack of clarity, visibility, and authority.

That's when I found the line that became my life's work—a simple promise:

"My job is to make you enter the room before you enter the room."

This book is that promise, in your hands.

This is not theory. Not corporate jargon. Not another list of content tips.

This is a mirror.

A guide.

A mentor in print.

A toolkit for transformation.

...Designed to do one thing: help you stand out in a world that rewards only those who are seen. Within these pages, you will learn:

- What personal branding actually is (it's not what you think).
- Why is it the single greatest leverage point for your business today?
- How to discover your unshakeable positioning.
- How to shape perception and build undeniable authority.
- The exact system to become unforgettable.
- How to build a commanding personal brand in 120 days.
- How to shift the way the world sees you-for good.

This is your step-by-step blueprint to becoming the person you were always meant to be. If you're ready to be seen-truly seen-not for your logo, but for your legacy…

Turn the page.

Your story starts now.

CHAPTER 1

The Revolution of Solar Pumping in India

The Quiet Revolution Changing Everything

> *"Personal branding is the art of becoming knowable, likable, and trustable."*
> ***- John Jantsch***

There's a question that haunts every business owner I've ever met. It's not about cash flow or competition or scaling. It's more fundamental than that.

It's the question you ask yourself in the quiet moment after a client chooses someone else. It's the question that surfaces when you're introduced as "the owner of that company" instead of by your name. It's the question that echoes in the gap between what you know you're worth and what the market seems willing to pay.

"Does anyone truly see me?"

Sometimes naming the question is the first step.

For twenty years, I watched this question play out in the lives of remarkable people. The manufacturer whose quality was unparalleled but whose name was unknown beyond his city. The consultant whose insights transformed businesses but who struggled to fill her calendar. The doctor whose healing touch was legendary but whose waiting room wasn't.

And I realized something that changed everything:

- We are living through a silent revolution.
- A revolution where perception has become more powerful than product.
- Where visibility has become more valuable than inventory.
- Where who you are matters more than what you sell.

The Day Everything Changed for Rohan

Let me tell you about Rohan Mehta (name changed for privacy).

Third-generation owner of a precision engineering unit in Pune. His grandfather started it, his father grew it, and he modernized it. Their components were in machines across three continents.

- The quality? **Impeccable.**
- The business? **Profitable.**
- The reputation? **Anonymous.**

One Tuesday morning, Rohan lost a $200,000 order.

- ➔ Not to a German competitor with better technology.
- ➔ Not to a Chinese factory with lower prices.

He lost it to a startup founder in Bangalore who had been posting about manufacturing innovation on LinkedIn for eighteen months.

- ➔ A founder whose factory was one-tenth the size of Rohan's.
- ➔ A founder whose technical knowledge was a fraction of Rohan's.

But here's what that founder had that Rohan didn't:

- A face.
- A story.
- A voice that preceded him into the room.

When the client Googled both of them, here's what they found:

Rohan: A sparse LinkedIn profile, last updated in 2017.

The other founder:

- Eighty-three articles on the future of Indian manufacturing.
- Thirty-seven videos explaining complex processes simply.
- Testimonials from respected industry leaders.
- A clear, compelling narrative about revolutionizing precision engineering.

The client didn't choose the better manufacturer.

They chose the better-known manufacturer.

That Tuesday broke something in Rohan.

But it also awakened something.

What Personal Branding Really Is (And What It's Not)

Let's clear the confusion right now.

Personal branding is not:

- Becoming an "Influencer."
- Posting selfies with motivational quotes.
- Creating a fake, perfect online persona.
- Shouting into the void of social media.
- Turning your life into content.

That's performance. That's exhaustion. That's building a mask.

Real personal branding is something entirely different.

It's the intentional alignment of three things:

- Who you truly are (your values, strengths, story).
- What you uniquely offer (your expertise, your approach).
- How the world perceives you (your reputation, your visibility).

It's the bridge between your internal truth and your external impact.

Think of the most respected people in your industry. Not the loudest, but the most respected. When you hear their name, what comes to mind?

Not just their company. Not just their title.

Them. Their integrity. Their insight. Their way of being.

That's personal branding in its purest form.

A Simple Definition That Changes Everything

Strip away all the jargon. Forget the marketing speak.

Here's what personal branding actually is:

Personal branding is the practice of consistently showing up as your most authentic, valuable self, so clearly that the right people can't help but notice, remember, and choose you.

It's not about being different.

It's about being distinctly you.

It's not about being everywhere.

It's about being found by the right people, in the right way.

It's not about shouting louder than everyone else.

It's about speaking so truly that the noise doesn't matter.

The Three Lies That Keep You Invisible

Before we go further, we need to dismantle the myths that keep capable people hidden:

Lie #1: "My work should speak for itself."

In a world of infinite noise, silent excellence is invisible excellence. Your work can only speak if people are listening. Personal branding is turning up the volume on your value.

Lie #2: "This is self-promotion, and that feels wrong."

There's a profound difference between self-promotion (shouting "Look at me!") and value-sharing (whispering "This might help you"). One comes from the ego. The other comes from generosity.

Lie #3: "I need to be perfect before I put myself out there."

Perfection is the enemy of progress. The most compelling personal brands aren't perfect—they're human. They share struggles, lessons learned, and real-time growth. That's what creates connection.

Your Personal Brand Already Exists

Here's the truth you might not want to hear:

You already have a personal brand.

Right now, as you read this, people have perceptions about you. Your clients. Your team. Your peers. Your competitors.

When someone hears your name, they feel something. They think something. They remember something.

The question isn't: "Do I have a personal brand?"

The question is: "Am I actively shaping my personal brand, or am I letting accident and assumption shape it for me?"

- Your digital footprint tells a story.
- Your conversations tell a story.
- Your work tells a story.

The only choice you have is **whether that story is intentional or accidental.**

A Moment of Honest Reflection

Pause here for just sixty seconds.

- Think of the last time you felt underestimated.
- The last time you had to justify your price.
- The last time someone didn't recognize the depth of your experience.

Now ask yourself:

Was that about my capability? Or was that about my visibility?

That feeling in your gut as you answer, that's your compass.

That's what tells you whether this journey is for you.

Because personal branding isn't about becoming famous.

It's about becoming findable to the people who need what only you can offer.

It's about ensuring that the next time opportunity knocks, it's knocking on your door, not because you shouted the loudest, but because you built thc most trustworthy home.

This is where your visibility journey begins.

Not with a strategy, but with a realization:

That in today's world, being seen isn't vanity, it's a responsibility.

- To your business.
- To your team.
- To your legacy.
- To yourself.

Turn the page when you're ready to see what happens when this realization remains unrealized.

CHAPTER 2

Who Is Personal Branding For?

The Quiet Crisis of the Capable

Let me tell you about three people. You might recognize yourself in one of them.

Arvind: The Industry's Best Kept Secret

Arvind runs a **45-year-old family textile business in Surat.**

His grandfather started with one loom. His father built the first factory. Arvind automated production, expanded to exports, and survived three economic downturns.

His **quality is a benchmark** in itself. His **word is bond.**

His reputation & visibility? Well, that is another story; it ends at the factory gate.

When international buyers visit Surat, they meet his flashier competitors first, while Arvind keeps waiting for referrals.

He's the industry's best-kept secret.

Priya: The Offline Lawyer

Priya is a corporate lawyer who left her partnership to start her own practice.

She's sharper than anyone in the room. She understands contract nuance like a poet understands meter. Her clients get results.

However, her practice grows slowly, case by case, introduction by introduction.

She watches younger, less experienced lawyers build thriving practices online.

They're **not better** lawyers. But they're **better-known** lawyers.

Dr. Gaurav Kapoor: The Invisible Doctor

Dr. Kapoor is a renowned cardiologist in Delhi.

His hands have saved thousands of lives.

His colleagues respect him.

His patients revere him.

However, whenever the media needs a heart health expert, they call the doctor who writes a newspaper column.

When medical conferences need a speaker, they invite the doctor with the YouTube channel.

Dr. Kapoor's expertise is in depth, but his visibility is shallow.

- ➢ Three different industries.
- ➢ Three different stories.

One identical problem:

- ➔ They built exceptional skill, but forgot to build an exceptional presence.
- ➔ They believed competence was enough.
- ➔ They believed reputation would travel on its own.
- ➔ They believed being the best meant being chosen first.

And every single day, in quiet moments, they feel the gap between their capability and their recognition.

The Unspoken Truth About "For Whom"

Most personal branding advice gets this wrong. It talks about demographics: **"for entrepreneurs," "for professionals," "for creators."**

But personal branding isn't for a category of person.

It's for a state of being.

It's for anyone who has ever felt this specific frustration:

"I know I'm good at what I do. Why doesn't everyone else know it too?"

It's for the people who are tired of:

- ➢ Explaining their value from scratch every single time
- ➢ Watching lesser competitors win because they're louder
- ➢ Having their price questioned despite their expertise
- ➢ Being the last to know about industry opportunities
- ➢ Feeling like their success is always one referral away from disappearing

If you've ever delivered work that made you proud, then watched the credit go to someone more visible, this chapter is your validation.

The Seven Archetypes of the Invisible Expert

Through my work, I've seen seven patterns emerge. See where you fit:

1. The Legacy Builder

You've built something substantial, a business, a practicc, a portfolio. It has weight. It has history. But it doesn't have your face on it. You're known for what you built, not for who you are as its builder.

2. The Quiet Specialist

Your expertise runs deep. You know things that few others do. You solve problems others can't. But your knowledge is a well that no one knows exists. People drink from noisier, shallower wells instead.

3. The Transitional Leader

You're taking over a family business. Or stepping into a leadership role. Or pivoting your career. You have big shoes to fill, but you're standing in someone else's shadow. You need your own light.

4. The Value Creator

You consistently deliver exceptional results. Your clients are happy. Your work speaks for itself. But it only speaks to the people already in the room. You need it to speak to the people who haven't arrived yet.

5. The Industry Insider

You know everyone in your field. They respect you. But outside your immediate circle? Silence. You have influence without reach, respect without recognition.

6. The Modern Professional

Doctors, lawyers, architects, consultants. Your credentials are impeccable. Your experience is vast. But in a digital world, you're competing with people who've made their expertise public property. Your private excellence is losing to their public authority.

7. The Purpose-Driven Creator

Coaches, healers, artists, teachers. Your work is your calling. It comes from your soul. But souls don't market themselves. And the people who need your gift most might never find it if you remain hidden.

The Most Dangerous Myth of All

There's a belief that stops more talented people than any lack of skill ever could.

It's the belief that says:

"If I just keep getting better, eventually I'll be discovered."

This is the "field of dreams" fallacy: build it, and they will come.

Except they won't.

- Not anymore.
- Not in a world where everyone is building and everyone is shouting.

Waiting to be discovered is not a strategy.

- It's surrender.
- It's surrendering your narrative to chance.
- It's surrendering your opportunities to luck.
- It's surrendering your value to the mercy of others' attention.

The Real Question Isn't "Is This For Me?"

By now, you know if personal branding is for you.

Your gut has already answered.

The real question, the one that matters, is:

"What version of myself am I willing to become?"

Because personal branding isn't about adding something new to who you are.

It's about revealing more of who you already are to more of the people who need to see it.

It's not transformation. It's transparency.

A Moment of Clear Seeing

Look at your hands.

These hands have built things. Solved problems. Created value.

Now look at your phone.

Open LinkedIn. Search your name.

What do those hands look like to someone who doesn't know you?

Do they see the calluses of experience?

The steadiness of expertise?

The fingerprints of your unique way of working?

Or do they see… nothing?

That gap—between what your hands have actually done and what the digital world shows they've done—that's the territory we're about to reclaim.

The Simple, Unavoidable Truth

In the next decade, there will be two kinds of professionals:

Those who are findable.

And those who are forgotten.

Those who shape perception.

And those who are shaped by it.

Those who build visibility intentionally.

And those who experience invisibility accidentally.

This isn't a prediction.

This is already happening.

The question isn't whether you need a personal brand.

The question is how long you can afford not to have one.

Your Turning Point

If you've read this far, something has already shifted.

You might feel a slight discomfort. That's good.

Growth begins just outside your comfort zone.

You might feel resistance. That's normal.

We protect what's familiar, even when it's not serving us.

But underneath that, if you feel a spark, a quiet "what if?" Then pay attention.

That spark is your future self, whispering.

This chapter isn't ending with answers.

It's ending with a choice.

➔ You can close this book and return to the familiar struggle of being good but unknown.

→ Or you can turn the page and discover what happens when good people decide to become impossible to ignore.

The capable have been invisible long enough.

Your time to be seen starts now.

If this chapter felt uncomfortably familiar, you're not alone.

Scan to watch people share what changed when they finally stepped forward.

CHAPTER 3

The Invisible Tax

What Your Silence is Costing You

There's a quiet transaction happening in your business right now. You don't see it on your P&L. You won't find it in your balance sheet. But it's real. **And it's costing you more than you've ever calculated.**

I call it The Invisible Tax, the compound interest you pay for being unknown.

Let me show you how it works, not in theory, but in the language you understand best: numbers, time, and opportunity.

The Monday That Changed Everything for Sameer

Sameer Shah ran a packaging solutions company in Ahmedabad for twelve years. Good clientele. Steady growth.

He believed in the old ways:

- Work hard.
- Deliver quality.
- Keep your head down.

One Monday morning, his biggest client, a FMCG brand he'd served for eight years, called.

Not to place an order, but to inform him they were moving 70% of their business to a new vendor.

"Their pricing is better?" Sameer asked, already mentally calculating how low he could go.

"Actually, they're 15% more expensive," the client said.

"But their founder has been consulting with us on sustainability packaging for six months. He's become our go-to expert. We trust his vision."

Sameer hung up the phone.

The competitor wasn't better at packaging.

He was better at being known for packaging.

That Monday, Sameer didn't just lose an account.

He paid the invisible tax.

And the bill was ₹3.2 crores in annual revenue.

The Seven Line Items of the Invisible Tax

Most business owners track every expense.

But they miss the seven most costly ones:

1. The Opportunity Tax

What you lose by not being top of mind.

Every day, opportunities pass by your silent door: partnerships, media features, investor interest, talent acquisition. They flow to visible people. You pay with missed growth.

2. The Trust Tax

What you spend building credibility from zero.

When you're unknown, every new relationship starts at -10. You spend meetings proving you're legitimate instead of discussing how you can help. You pay with time and energy you'll never get back.

3. The Pricing Tax

The gap between what you're worth and what you can charge.

Without authority, your price is always negotiable. You leave 15-30% on the table with every deal. Do the math: if your business does ₹5 crores annually, that's ₹75 lakhs to ₹1.5 crores in pure margin, gone.

4. The Speed Tax

The extra time it takes to close everything.

Visible experts close deals in one meeting. You need three. Their proposals get reviewed in days. Yours wait for weeks. You pay with elongated sales cycles and mental exhaustion.

5. The Talent Tax

The premium you pay for average people.

Top talent follows visible leaders. When you're invisible, you don't get the superstar employee who emails you saying, "I believe in your mission." You get the person who responds to your job ad. You pay with mediocrity.

6. The Referral Tax

The limitation of growth by word-of-mouth alone.

Referrals are beautiful, but they're finite. They depend on your network's memory and motivation. When you're invisible beyond your circle, your growth ceiling is someone else's social capital. You pay with capped potential.

7. The Legacy Tax

What disappears when you're not the face of your work?

You build a business that could survive without you, but will anyone remember why it mattered? Legacy isn't about exit value; it's about enduring impact. You pay with anonymity.

The Cumulative Cost: A Year in the Life

Let's make this painfully concrete. Take "A," a capable business owner with ₹10 crores in revenue:

Invisible Tax Line Item	Annual Cost (A Conservative Estimate)
Lost premium clients	₹1.5 crores
Discounted pricing	₹1.2 crores
Extended sales cycles	₹75 lakhs (opportunity cost)
Recruitment compromises	₹50 lakhs
Missed partnerships	₹2 crores
Total Annual Tax	**₹5.95 crores**

That's not revenue. That's leakage.

Money, opportunity, and potential slipping through the cracks of your invisibility.

The worst part? You've probably budgeted for this.

You've accepted it as "the cost of doing business."

But it's not. It's the cost of not being seen doing business.

The Psychological Toll (The Interest on the Tax)

The financial cost is calculable. The human cost is where it becomes painful.

I've sat with hundreds of business owners in their moments of quiet frustration. The pattern is always the same:

"I know I'm good at this. I've spent years getting good at this. Why do I still have to convince people?"

This isn't just business stress. This is identity erosion.

- Every time you justify your worth, a piece of your confidence chips away.

- Every time a less capable competitor wins, a doubt takes root.
- Every time you're introduced as "what you do" instead of "who you are," your sense of self diminishes.

You start playing smaller. Charging less. Dreaming narrower.

Not because your capability decreased, but because your visibility never increased.

The Visibility Window

Here's what most people miss: invisibility isn't static. It's progressive.

Like vision fading slowly, you don't notice the dimming until you can barely see.

- **Year 1:** You're new. Invisibility is expected.
- **Year 3:** You're established, but unknown. Opportunities pass by.
- **Year 5:** You're capable but overlooked. Frustration builds.
- **Year 10:** You're respected in your circle but invisible beyond it. Growth plateaus.
- **Year 15:** You're the industry's secret weapon. And secrets don't scale.

The longer you wait, the higher the invisible tax compounds.

And the harder it becomes to change the narrative.

The Alternative: A Different Monday For Sameer

Let's return to Sameer six months later.

After losing that client, he committed to one hour a day, three days a week, to building his visibility.

Not selling, but teaching. Sharing what he knew about sustainable packaging.

- He wrote one LinkedIn article weekly.
- He recorded short videos explaining industry shifts.
- He started a simple newsletter for his clients.

One Monday morning, six months in, his phone rang.

It was a European retail giant expanding into India.

"We've been reading your insights on circular economy packaging," their head of sustainability said. "We need a partner who understands this at your level.

Can you consult on our India launch?"

The **project fee: ₹85 lakhs.**

The time from first contact to signed contract: just eleven days.

Sameer didn't just recover his lost revenue.

He discovered a new revenue line he never knew existed.

The tax he'd been paying became an investment that paid him back 10x.

Your Personal Tax Assessment

Take sixty seconds. Be brutally honest.

- How many premium clients have you lost to more visible competitors?
- What discount do you typically give to win business?
- How many weeks does your average sales cycle take?
- What opportunities came to someone else because they were more top-of-mind?
- What brilliant hire didn't join you because they'd never heard of you?

The sum of those answers isn't theoretical.

It's your current invisible tax rate.

And here's the liberating truth:

This isn't a permanent condition.

It's a changeable variable.

The Turning Point

There comes a moment in every leader's journey when the cost of staying silent becomes greater than the fear of being seen.

For Sameer, it was a ₹3.2 crore loss.

For you, it might be something else.

- Maybe it's watching your twentieth proposal get negotiated down.
- Maybe it's seeing a younger competitor get the industry award you deserved.
- Maybe it's the quiet realization that you've built everything except your own reputation.

That moment, when frustration finally outweighs fear, is your turning point.

You've just completed your personal tax audit.

You've seen the real cost of invisibility.

The next chapter isn't about more costs.

It's about proof, evidence that building visibility isn't just damage control, but the most powerful growth accelerator available to you today.

Turn the page when you're ready to see what happens when the tax ends and the investment begins.

The cost of invisibility isn't theoretical.

Scan to watch how others stopped paying it—and what shifted next.

CHAPTER 3

The Invisible Tax

What Your Silence is Costing You

In 2018, something quiet happened in a boardroom in South Mumbai that changed how I understood everything.

A fifth-generation family business was considering a new CEO. The choice was between two candidates:

Candidate A: Ivy League MBA, 20 years at multinationals, impeccable credentials, flawless resume.

Candidate B: Local MBA, 15 years mostly in family businesses, less polished on paper.

The board was leaning toward Candidate A. Then one director did what everyone now does: **he Googled them.**

Candidate A: Corporate headshots. Standard LinkedIn. Dry articles in trade journals.

Candidate B:

- A thoughtful series on "Modernizing Legacy Businesses" with 50,000+ views.
- Videos speaking about ethical leadership.
- Podcast interviews about balancing tradition with innovation.
- A clear, compelling narrative about the future of Indian family enterprises.

The board hired Candidate B.

When asked why, the chairman said something I'll never forget:

"We're not just hiring skills. We're hiring a story.

And his story was already being told."

This wasn't intuition.

- This was evidence-based decision-making in its most modern form.
- The data was clear: the candidate who controlled his narrative controlled his destiny.

The Harvard Study That Changed Leadership Forever

Researchers at Harvard Business School spent three years tracking 500 companies during leadership transitions. They weren't studying products or strategies. They were studying visibility.

Their finding was startling:

➔ Companies where incoming leadership had established public visibility before taking over saw 23% higher shareholder returns in their first year.

The reason?

- Trust transferred faster.
- Markets reacted positively.
- Employees felt more secure.
- Stakeholders understood the vision immediately.

The study concluded:

"In the digital age, leadership is no longer a private role. It is a public narrative.

Those who shape that narrative before assuming a position gain immediate credibility and momentum."

Translation: Visibility isn't just about getting opportunities.

It's about multiplying the impact of every opportunity you get.

The LinkedIn Revelation

LinkedIn's internal data team discovered something their own platform was making inevitable:

Content posted by individual employees receives 8x more engagement than content posted by company pages.

But here's the more important finding:

When those employees had consistent personal brands, clear positioning, and regular, valuable content, their engagement jumped to 14x company page levels.

The platform's own conclusion?

"The era of faceless corporations is ending. The era of visible leaders has begun."

- Your company page is your brochure.
- Your personal profile is your handshake with the future.

The Indian MSME Study: When Silence Becomes Expensive

A 2022 study by an Indian business school focused specifically on our context. **Researchers tracked 200 MSMEs across Gujarat, Maharashtra, and Tamil Nadu for two years.**

They divided them into two groups:

Group A: Founders with no digital presence

Group B: Founders with consistent professional visibility (LinkedIn articles, industry talks, clear personal positioning)

After 24 months:

Metric	Group A (Silent)	Group B (Visible)
Average revenue growth	12%	34%
Premium pricing acceptance	41%	78%
Talent attraction rate	2.1 applications per role	8.7 applications per role
Partnership opportunities	0.8 per year	3.4 per year
Media/investor inbound	0.3 per year	2.9 per year

The study's lead researcher summarized:

"In India's competitive MSME landscape, founder visibility has emerged as the single most underutilized competitive advantage. It's not replacing product quality, it's amplifying it."

The Doctor Who Broke the Mold

Dr. Ananya Mehta didn't set out to become "visible." **She just wanted to help more patients.**

A dermatologist in Bangalore, she watched patients struggle with misinformation online.

So she started recording 90-second videos explaining common skin conditions in simple terms.

No fancy production. Just her phone, good lighting, and clarity.

In six months:

- Her clinic's waiting time went from 2 days to 2 weeks
- 40% of new patients mentioned her videos
- She was invited to speak at three medical conferences
- Pharmaceutical companies approached her for ethical partnerships

But here's the data point that matters most:

Her patient adherence rate (following treatment plans) increased by 65%.

Why?

- Because patients who found her through her educational content already trusted her expertise.
- They weren't just buying a consultation; they were buying into her guidance system.

Dr. Mehta proved something critical:

In expert fields, visibility isn't marketing.

It's pre-education that makes every subsequent interaction more effective.

The Psychology Behind the Numbers

Why does this work? It's not magic. It's human wiring.

1. The Mere-Exposure Effect

Psychologists have proven that we develop a preference for things merely because we're familiar with them. When people see your face, hear your ideas, and recognize your name repeatedly, they unconsciously begin to trust you. Familiarity breeds not contempt, but comfort.

2. The Halo Effect

When we admire one quality in someone, we tend to assume they have other positive qualities. A founder who clearly explains industry complexities is assumed to be competent in execution. A doctor who educates well is assumed to be skilled in treatment. Visibility creates a positive presumption.

3. Social Proof at Scale

When others engage with your content—liking, sharing, commenting—it signals to newcomers: "This person is worth paying attention to." It's the digital equivalent of a crowded restaurant looking more appealing than an empty one.

The Manufacturing Case Study: From Vendor to Visionary

Rohit Malhotra ran a component manufacturing unit in Noida for 17 years. He was good, really good.

But he was a vendor, not a partner.

Then he started writing one article per month on LinkedIn about "The Future of Indian Manufacturing." Not sales pitches.

Real insights about automation, skilled labor, and quality standards. In eight months:

- Two German companies approached him for sourcing partnerships
- An industrial publication asked him to write a regular column
- He was invited to join a government advisory panel on MSME modernization
- His pricing power increased by 22% without negotiation

But here's what Rohit told me that matters more than any number:

"For the first time, clients stopped asking me to justify my costs.

They started asking me to guide their strategy."

That shift, from cost center to strategic partner, is the real ROI of visibility.

The Global Pattern

This isn't an Indian phenomenon. It's a human phenomenon in the digital age.

- **In the US:** Consultants with established thought leadership command 3-5x higher fees.
- **In Europe:** Family business successors with public visibility smooth transitions and maintain stakeholder confidence.
- **In Southeast Asia:** Professionals who share expertise become regional go-to experts, expanding their market reach exponentially.

The pattern is universal:

Visibility creates velocity.

Authority creates advantage.

Your Evidence File

By now, you might be thinking of exceptions. "But what about…?"

Let me save you the mental energy:

For every "exception" of someone succeeding in silence, there are hundreds of visible people succeeding faster, bigger, and with more impact.

The evidence isn't just in studies. It's in:

- The founder who closes deals before meetings start
- The professional who gets inbound inquiries daily
- The expert whose opinion shapes industry conversations
- The leader whose team recruits itself

This isn't speculation. This is an observable reality in today's business landscape.

The Question That Matters Now

The data is clear. The case studies are compelling. The psychology is proven.

So the question shifts from

"Does this work?"

to:

"What am I going to do with this information?"

You now stand at the intersection of evidence and action.

You can acknowledge the data and return to business as usual.

Or you can recognize that you've been handed the operating manual for modern influence.

- You've seen the proof.
- You've understood the psychology.
- You've witnessed the transformations.

The next chapter isn't about more evidence.

It's about mechanism, exactly how visibility translates into tangible business outcomes.

Turn the page when you're ready to understand the engine, not just admire the car.

Data explains. Experience convinces.

Scan to watch real people talk about how visibility changed their trajectory.

CHAPTER 5

The Mechanism

How Visibility Becomes Velocity

Let me tell you about a factory in Rajkot.

Not the machinery. Not the output. The conversations.

A Pivotal Shift in Perception & Conversation

For twenty-three years, the owner, Vikram Patel, had one kind of conversation with clients.

This is what they would say to him:

- "What's your best price?"
- "Can you deliver faster?"
- "What's your MOQ?"

Then, something shifted.

After Vikram began sharing his knowledge about precision engineering, not selling, just teaching, the conversations changed:

- "How would you solve this tolerance issue?"
- "What's your take on automation for small batches?"
- "Can you consult on our production line redesign?"

Same factory. Same man. Same expertise.

Different value perception.

This shift from product provider to problem-solver didn't happen by chance. It happened through a specific, repeatable mechanism.

A mechanism that turns visibility into business velocity.

The Three-Phase Conversion Engine

Visibility doesn't magically create business. It creates the conditions for business to happen easily, quickly, and profitably.

Here's how the engine works:

Phase 1: The Attention Filter

Visibility separates signal from noise.

When you're invisible, you compete in the noise. Everyone shouts. Buyers filter by price.

When you're visible with valuable insights, you become the signal in their noise. You don't fight for attention; you earn it by providing value first.

Real-World Translation: Your LinkedIn article about sustainable manufacturing doesn't just get likes. It gets saved by a plant head researching solutions. When they need a vendor six months later, whose name comes to mind first?

Phase 2: The Trust Accelerator

Visibility compresses time.

Trust typically builds through repeated interactions: meetings, calls, referrals, and proofs.

Visibility creates pre-built trust. Your content becomes those interactions happening at scale, before you ever meet.

The Math of Compressed Time:

- Traditional trust-building: 3 meetings + 2 calls + 1 reference check = 6-8 weeks
- Visibility-accelerated: 8 articles read + 5 videos watched + social proof observed = Trust built before first meeting

Phase 3: The Value Amplifier

Visibility reframes your worth.

When you're unknown, your value is measured against competitors' pricing.

When you're known as an expert, your value is measured against the cost of not solving the problem. This is the difference between "Your price is high" and "Your solution is worth it."

The Ripple Effect

How One Piece of Content Creates Multiple Opportunities

Most business owners think linearly: Post content → Get noticed → Maybe get business.

But visibility works in ripples, not straight lines.

Let me show you with Rina Sharma's story:

Rina's Ripples

Rina ran a boutique HR consultancy. She wrote one detailed LinkedIn article: "Why Your Best Employees Are Quietly Quitting (And What to Actually Do About It)."

- **Ripple 1:** The article got 42,000 views. Good, but not the point.
- **Ripple 2:** A talent acquisition head at a unicorn startup DMed her: "This articulated what I've been feeling. Can we talk?"
- **Ripple 3:** That conversation led to a consulting project.
- **Ripple 4:** She mentioned the project (generically) in a follow-up article.
- **Ripple 5:** Two more companies reached out based on that mention.
- **Ripple 6:** One of those companies asked her to speak at their leadership offsite.
- **Ripple 7:** At the offsite, she met a venture capitalist.
- **Ripple 8:** The VC asked her to consult on portfolio company culture.

One article. Eight business opportunities.

Not because she was "viral," but because she was valuable consistently.

The Permission Paradox

Here's what most people miss: Visibility doesn't just bring opportunities. It gives you permission.

Permission to:

- Charge premium fees (because you're perceived as premium)
- Set boundaries (because you're in demand)

- Choose your clients (because they're coming to you)
- Speak truth (because you've earned authority)
- Innovate (because you're seen as a forward-thinker)

Without visibility, you ask for permission.

With visibility, you are granted permission.

The Competitor Immunity

When you become the visible expert in your space, something remarkable happens: you stop competing. Not because there's no competition, but because you're no longer in the same category. **Think about it:**

- Generic contractors compete on price.
- "The sustainability-focused construction expert" doesn't compete with them.
- Generic consultants compete on deliverables.
- "The digital transformation guide for family businesses" exists in a different conversation.

Visibility allows you to redefine the competition by redefining the category.

The Talent Magnet Effect

Ajay ran a software development firm for eight years. He posted job ads. He paid recruiters. He got applicants who needed jobs.

Then he started sharing his philosophy on building engineering teams that last. Not recruiting tips, his actual beliefs about mentorship, growth, and culture.

Within three months:

- 4 senior engineers reached out directly
- A product manager from a FAANG company asked about opportunities
- His existing team shared his content proudly
- Employee referral quality increased by 300%

Ajay discovered: **Visibility attracts not just clients, but co-creators.**

People don't just want to work **for** visible leaders.

They want to work **with** them.

The Pricing Algorithm Shift

Here's the most financially significant mechanism:

Traditional Pricing: Cost + Margin + Market Comparison = Your Price

Visibility-Driven Pricing: Problem Value + Your Unique Insight + Proof of Results = Your Price

Let me make this concrete with numbers:

Traditional Scenario:

- Client has a ₹50 lakh problem
- You quote ₹15 lakhs as a consultant
- Client negotiates to ₹12 lakhs
- You accept (24% discount)

Visibility-Driven Scenario:

- Same ₹50 lakh problem
- Client has read your framework for solving exactly this

- You quote ₹20 lakhs (40% of problem value, not your cost)
- Client accepts (they're buying certainty, not hours)

The difference isn't just ₹8 lakhs.

It's pricing based on delivered value rather than delivered time.

The Compound Interest of Consistency

One post is a transaction.

Consistent visibility is an investment that compounds.

- **Month 1:** A few people notice you.
- **Month 3:** People recognize your name.
- **Month 6:** People anticipate your insights.
- **Month 12:** People cite your thinking.
- **Month 24:** You shape the conversation.

This isn't hype. This is a mathematical inevitability when valuable consistency meets time.

The Mechanism in Your Hands

By now, you understand this isn't about "getting famous."

It's about activating a business growth mechanism that:

- Filters for quality opportunities
- Accelerates trust-building
- Amplifies your perceived value
- Attracts ideal clients and talent
- Repositions you above price competition
- Compounds over time

The mechanism exists. It's proven. It's waiting.

Your Turning Point

There's a moment in every implementation where theory becomes practice. Where understanding becomes action. That moment happens when you move from "This makes sense" to "This is how I'll implement it."

You now have the blueprint for the most powerful business growth mechanism available today. Not a marketing tactic.

Not a social media strategy.

A fundamental recalibration of how value is created, communicated, and captured in the digital age.

The mechanism is clear.

The path is illuminated.

The evidence is overwhelming.

The next question is personal:

What part of your business deserves this acceleration first?

Turn the page when you're ready to build the foundation.

CHAPTER 6

The Foundation

What You Build Before You Build

There is a moment in construction that fascinates me more than the finished building.

It's not when the first brick is laid.

It's what happens before, when the ground is cleared, measured, and marked. When invisible lines decide everything that comes after.

That moment, the foundation determines whether what you build stands for decades or collapses under its own weight.

For twenty years, I watched brilliant business owners make one critical mistake:

They built incredible companies on invisible foundations.

They poured their genius into products, services, systems, all standing on ground nobody could see.

And then they wondered why their structures felt unstable.

Why did recognition not come?

Why did their value seem to disappear into the earth?

This chapter is about doing what should have been done first.

It's about building the visible foundation that makes everything else not just possible, but permanent.

The Three Invisible Truths You Must Make Visible

Before you create content, before you choose platforms, before you think about "branding", you must excavate and elevate three fundamental truths.

Truth #1: Your Origin Story

Not what you do, but why you do it this way.

Most business owners tell their story like a resume:

"I started in 2008, we expanded in 2012, we added services in 2015…"

Your origin story isn't dates. It's decisions.

Take Meena, who runs a chain of preschools. Her "origin story" used to be:

"I started Little Stars in 2010 with two centers; now we have twelve."

Then she excavated deeper.

- ➔ She remembered sitting in a corporate job, watching her niece come home from preschool with worksheets instead of wonder.
- ➔ She remembered the moment she decided children should learn through curiosity, not compliance.

That became her origin story:

"I left corporate America when I realized our education system was teaching compliance instead of curiosity.

Every preschool I build is a rebellion against worksheets and a revolution toward wonder."

See the difference?

One is facts.

The other is **the** foundation.

Your Exercise:

- ➔ What decision, not what date, truly started your journey?
- ➔ What problem did you refuse to accept anymore?
- ➔ What belief made you leave the well-trodden path?

Truth #2: Your Signature Strength

Not what you're good at, but how you're uniquely good at it.

Every business owner has skills. But skills can be copied.

Your signature strength is how you apply those skills in a way nobody else does.

Consider two architects:

Architect A: "I design sustainable buildings."

Architect B: "I design buildings that remember they're on Indian soil, using ancient cooling techniques with modern materials, creating spaces that feel like they've always belonged here."

One has a skill. The other has a philosophy made visible.

Your Exercise:

Complete this sentence:

"Yes, others do [your service], but I'm the one who…"

The answer isn't "does it better." It's "approaches it differently because…"

Truth #3: Your Audience's Unspoken Question

Not what they ask, but what they're afraid to ask.

Your ideal clients have surface questions:

- "What's your price?"
- "How long will it take?"
- "Can you show examples?"

But beneath those questions lies the real one:

➔ "Can I trust you with this?"

Your foundation must answer that unspoken question before it's asked.

The Visibility Blueprint: One Page That Changes Everything

I want you to create something now. Not in your mind. On paper.

One page. Three sections.

Section A: My Visible Anchor

(The Story That Holds Everything) In three sentences:

- The problem I witnessed that broke my heart/angered me/ frustrated me
- The moment I decided to build a different way
- The single belief that guides every decision I make

Section B: My Distinctive Ground

(What Makes My Soil Different) Complete these:

- I believe _____, even when others believe _____
- I always _____, even when it would be easier to _____
- What looks like _____ to others looks like _____ to me

Section C: The Bridge I Build

(Connecting My Truth to Their Need) Answer for your ideal client:

- Before they find me, they believe _____
- After working with me, they understand _____
- The transformation isn't just _____; it's _____

This page isn't for posting.

It's for positioning.

It's the foundation upon which every post, every talk, every conversation will stand.

The Cost of Skipping This Step

I've seen what happens when brilliant people build visibility without a foundation.

- They create content that feels scattered.
- They attract the wrong opportunities.

- They burn out from constantly reinventing their message.
- They become another voice in the noise instead of a clear signal above it.

The foundation doesn't limit you.

It liberates you.

When you know your visible anchor, every decision becomes easier. When you understand your distinctive ground, every piece of content becomes coherent. When you've built your bridge, every conversation becomes meaningful.

The Architect Who Found His Ground

Rajiv was a brilliant architect who designed beautiful homes.

For years, his visibility efforts felt like shouting into the wind.

He posted project photos. Got some likes. Nothing changed.

Then we excavated his foundation.

His origin story wasn't about architecture school.

It was about growing up in a joint family in Jaipur, watching how spaces dictated relationships.

How the courtyard wasn't just architecture, it was family glue.

His signature strength wasn't "good design." It was "designing homes that recreate the intimacy of joint families for nuclear families."

His audience's unspoken question wasn't **"Can you design my house?"**

It was **"Can you design a house that feels like a home even when we're all busy?"**

With that foundation, everything changed.

His content became:

- "Why your dining table is the most important piece of furniture you'll own."
- "The 3 architectural mistakes that make families feel disconnected."
- "How to design a home that grows with your children's independence."

In six months, he stopped bidding for projects.

Clients began their conversations with:

"I read your article about family connection spaces.
That's exactly what we need."

The foundation didn't just make him visible.

It made him inevitable for the right clients.

Your Foundation Moment

Right now, you have two choices:

- Build on someone else's ground. Use trending formats, popular topics, and what everyone else is doing. Your visibility will be temporary, exhausting, and easily washed away.
- Claim your own ground. Build on the bedrock of your authentic story, your distinctive approach, your genuine understanding of what your people need. Your visibility will become permanent, energizing, and magnetic.

The first choice gets quick results that fade.

The second choice builds something that lasts longer than you will.

The Question That Determines Everything

As you turn this page, ask yourself:

"What ground am I standing on that nobody else sees yet?"

That ground, that unique combination of your experience, your insight, your values, isn't just your foundation. It's your future.

And the moment you make it visible is the moment everything changes.

Your foundation awaits.

The ground is ready to be claimed.

The blueprint is in your hands.

The next chapter isn't about building higher.

It's about making what you've built impossible to ignore.

Turn the page when you're ready to enter rooms before you arrive.

If you're unsure how your foundation actually looks, we can talk.

sumit@iconicedge.org

CHAPTER 7

The Presence Principle

How to Enter Rooms Before You Arrive

The Meeting That Never Happened

Let me tell you about a meeting that never happened.

Two years ago, a client was considering me for a large personal branding project. Before our scheduled call, he did what everyone now does: he Googled me.

But he didn't just search "Sumit Kkhubchandani."

He searched "personal branding for family business succession."

- The first result was an article I'd written six months earlier.
- The second was a video where I interviewed a third-generation steel manufacturer.
- The third was a LinkedIn post breaking down a successful transition case.

He canceled our meeting.

Not because he wasn't interested, but because he was already convinced.

He emailed me:

"I've read your work. I understand your approach.

Let's skip the pitch and start with the contract."

That meeting didn't happen because I had already attended it.

My presence had entered the room months before I was invited.

This is the principle that changes everything:

In the digital age, your presence isn't where you are.

It's where your ideas have already traveled.

The Architecture of Presence

Presence isn't charisma. It's not being the loudest voice in the room.

It's something more subtle and powerful:

It's the gap between when someone needs expertise and when they discover you have it.

Most professionals wait for that gap to be filled by a meeting, a pitch, or a proposal.

Visible experts pre-fill that gap.

Think of it as building bridges before anyone asks to cross the river.

The Three Bridges Every Expert Must Build

Bridge 1: The Bridge of Recognition

Making sure people know what you solve before they have the problem.

A financial planner doesn't wait for someone to search "retirement planning."

She writes about "The 3 Money Mistakes 40-Year-Olds Make Without Realizing It."

When her ideal client turns 41 and realizes they need planning, whose name comes to mind?

The person who has already educated them about their blind spots.

Bridge 2: The Bridge of Credibility

Providing proof before being asked for it.

Testimonials on a website are reactive.

Case studies shared as teaching moments are proactive proof.

When a manufacturing consultant shares "How We Increased Output by 30% Without New Machinery," he's not just sharing a success story.

He's depositing credibility into an account that future clients will withdraw from.

Bridge 3: The Bridge of Approachability

Removing the fear of reaching out before the first contact.

The scariest email to write is: "I don't know you, but I need your help."

- But what if you've already shown your humanity?
- What if they've seen your video about failing at a project?
- What if they've read your honest take on industry challenges?
- Suddenly, you're not a stranger. You're the person who shares reality.

The Silent Handshake

Every piece of content you create is a handshake.

But unlike physical handshakes that happen once, these digital handshakes multiply.

One article about "Sustainable Practices for Small Factories" gets:

- Read by a factory owner in Coimbatore
- Shared with his operations head
- Saved by a consultant preparing for a client
- Cited in an industry report

- Found six months later by a journalist writing about sustainability

Your single handshake just met five people.

And the factory owner? He feels like he already knows you when you finally meet.

The Mumbai Lawyer Who Mastered Presence

Aditi practiced corporate law in Mumbai for fifteen years.

She was excellent but invisible beyond her immediate network.

Then she started building bridges.

Not by advertising her services.

By creating a simple newsletter: "3 Legal Insights for Indian Startups Each Month."

- Month 1: 47 subscribers.
- Month 3: 284 subscribers.
- Month 6: Over 1,000 subscribers.

But here's what matters:

In Month 7, she got an email from a startup founder:

"We're raising our Series A.

We've been reading your newsletter for six months.

We want you to lead our funding round legal work."

No pitch. No proposal. No "Can you send your credentials?"

Just: "We've learned from you already. Now we want to work with you."

Aditi didn't enter that room when she took the meeting.

She entered it the first time her newsletter landed in their inbox.

The Mathematics of Presence

Let's quantify what most people feel intuitively:

Traditional Approach:

1 meeting → 1 impression → Maybe 1 opportunity

Presence-First Approach:

1 article → 1,000 impressions → 100 reads → 10 saves → 3 shares → 1 referral → Multiple future opportunities

But the real math is more profound:

Time Saved Per Opportunity:

- **Traditional:** 3 meetings, 2 calls, 5 emails = 8+ hours
- **Presence-First:** 1 meeting = 1 hour

Trust Acceleration:

- **Traditional:** Built over weeks/months of interaction
- **Presence-First:** Pre-built through consumed content

Conversion Rate:

- **Traditional:** 20-30% for qualified leads
- **Presence-First:** 60-80% for inbound leads

The numbers reveal the truth:

Presence isn't an addition to your business development.

It's a multiplier of it.

The Four Pillars of Digital Presence

Building presence requires consistency in four areas:

1. Point of View

What do you believe that others overlook?

Not opinions. Informed perspectives backed by experience.

2. Generosity

What you give before being asked.

Your best ideas shared freely become your best marketing.

3. Consistency

Showing up even when no one seems to be watching.

Presence compounds through reliability.

4. Humanity

Showing the person behind the expertise.

Perfection creates distance. Humanity creates connection.

The CEO Who Became Inevitable

Rohan (name changed for privacy) took over his family's automotive parts business.

He was young. The industry veterans were skeptical.

Instead of trying to convince them in meetings, he built presence.

He started a YouTube channel explaining:

- The real cost of outdated manufacturing processes
- How Indian suppliers could compete globally
- The future of electric vehicle components in India

Within a year:

- Suppliers referred to him as "the young expert."
- International companies sought his opinion
- His pricing power increased by 40%
- He was invited to government policy discussions

Rohan didn't fight for a seat at the table.

He built his own table and watched others ask to join him.

Your Presence Audit

Take five minutes. Be honest.

- If someone Googled your name right now with your ideal client's problem, what would they find?
- What have you taught for free that proves your expertise?
- Where does your digital presence live when you're not actively promoting?
- What conversation are you consistently part of without being physically present?

The gap between your answers and "They'd find exactly what they need" is your presence gap.

And that gap is costing you more than you imagine.

The Most Powerful Realization

Presence isn't about being everywhere.

It's about being findable exactly when you're needed.

It's not shouting from rooftops.

It's leaving breadcrumbs that lead exactly to your door.

It's not competing for attention.

It's becoming the obvious answer before the question is fully asked.

Your Next Step

You don't need to be loud to have presence.

You need to be clear, consistent, and valuable in the places your ideal clients already look.

- One article.
- One zideo.
- One insight shared generously.

That's how you enter your next meeting before you schedule it.

That's how you become the obvious choice before the comparison begins.

That's how you build a business that comes to you instead of you chasing it.

Your presence isn't where you stand.

It's where your value has already landed.

The next chapter shows you how to build the system that makes this presence sustainable, scalable, and strategic. Turn the page when you're ready to move from principle to practice.

Presence shows up before you do.

Scan to watch how conversations, deals, and trust began before the first meeting.

CHAPTER 8

The Visibility System

From Random Acts to Reliable Results

Visibility isn't Random: It's Systematic

There is a factory in Faridabad that taught me everything about systems.

For three generations, they've produced precision components.

What fascinated me wasn't their output, but their input discipline.

- Every morning at 7 AM, the same quality of raw material arrives.
- Every machine undergoes maintenance at scheduled intervals, whether it needs it or not.
- Every component is measured against the same standards, every single time.

The owner told me:

"People see the products.

They don't see the system that makes the product quality inevitable."

That's when I realized:

Visibility without a system is like that factory without schedules, without standards, without discipline, producing sporadic results through heroic effort and constant stress.

Most professionals approach visibility like a hobbyist approaches a workshop: occasional bursts of inspiration, inconsistent effort, unpredictable outcomes.

This chapter is about building your visibility factory.

A system that makes being seen, remembered, and chosen not an event, but an output. Not something you do when you have time, but something that happens because you built the machinery.

The Four Machines in Your Visibility Factory

Every effective system has components that work together.

Your visibility system needs four machines running in harmony:

Machine 1: The Insight Refinery

Turning raw experience into a valuable perspective.

Most people have insights. They have "aha" moments in showers, during commutes, and in client meetings. And then... those insights evaporate.

Your Insight Refinery has three simple parts:

- A capture system (notes app, voice memos, physical notebook)
- A weekly refining session (30 minutes every Friday)
- An organization method (by theme, by audience, by format)

Example: A consultant notices clients consistently underestimate implementation timelines. That's a raw observation. The refinery turns it into: "The 3 Implementation Myths Even Smart Leaders Believe", an article, a carousel, a video script.

Machine 2: The Content Assembly Line

From one core idea to multiple deliverables.

The single biggest mistake is creating one piece at a time. The system creates clusters.

One core insight becomes:

- **Monday:** LinkedIn article
- **Wednesday:** Instagram carousel
- **Friday:** Email newsletter snippet
- **Following Monday:** Podcast talking points

You're not creating four pieces. You're repurposing one piece four ways.

Machine 3: The Distribution Network

Getting your work to the right eyes at the right time.

Posting and praying isn't distribution. It's hope.

Your distribution network knows:

- When your audience is most receptive (data, not guesswork)
- Which formats work where (articles on LinkedIn, stories on Instagram, deep dives in newsletters)
- How to sequence delivery for maximum impact

Machine 4: The Engagement Engine

Turning viewers into a community.

Likes are vanity. Comments are clues. Conversations are currency.

Your engagement engine has one rule:

For every piece you publish, spend twice as much time engaging with others' work.

Not random scrolling. Strategic engagement:

- Commenting on industry leaders' posts with value-added thoughts
- Responding to every comment on your own work
- Sharing others' work that complements your message

- Building genuine relationships, not accumulating transactions

The Two-Hour Weekly System

You don't need endless hours. You need strategic hours.

Here's the system I've seen work for CEOs, doctors, consultants, and business owners:

Sunday Evening (30 minutes):

- Review the week's insights captured
- Choose one core idea to build the week around
- Outline the content cluster

Monday Morning (45 minutes):

- Create the primary content piece (article or video)
- Schedule it

Wednesday Morning (30 minutes):

- Create the secondary format (carousel or newsletter)
- Engage with Monday's responses

Friday Morning (15 minutes):

Review the week's engagement

- Plan one strategic connection (comment on an industry leader's post, share someone's work meaningfully)

Two hours. One week. Consistent visibility.

The Accountant Who Systemized His Expertise

Vikram was a CA running a successful practice in Chennai.

He was always "too busy" for visibility.

Then he implemented the two-hour system.

His Insight Refinery captured client questions.

His Assembly Line turned "Common GST mistakes for e-commerce businesses" into:

- A detailed LinkedIn article
- A simple Instagram carousel
- A client email template
- A speaking topic for local business groups

In four months:

- His referral quality improved dramatically
- He started getting inquiries from outside Tamil Nadu
- He was invited to contribute to a national financial publication
- His practice revenue grew 35% without adding clients

Vikram didn't find more time.

He systemized the time he already had.

The Quality Control Dashboard

Every factory has quality checks. Your visibility system needs its own dashboard:

Weekly Metrics:

- Content published: ✓
- Strategic engagements: ✓
- New meaningful connections: ✓

Monthly Metrics:

- Inbound inquiries traceable to content: #
- Opportunities generated: #
- Audience growth (quality, not just quantity): ✓

Quarterly Reflection:

- What topics resonated most?
- What formats worked best?
- What relationships developed?
- What business outcomes resulted?

This isn't vanity metrics. This is strategic feedback that improves your system.

The Scalability Switch

Here's where most systems fail: they don't scale.

Your system must have a scalability switch, a way to increase output without a proportional increase in effort.

Scalability Levers:

- **Repurposing Depth:** One live talk becomes a video, transcript, article series, and email course.
- **Collaboration Amplification:** Partnering with complementary experts doubles reach without doubling work.
- **Template Efficiency:** Creating templates for recurring content types (case studies, how-to guides, opinion pieces).
- **Community Contribution:** Inviting your audience to contribute questions, stories, and perspectives.

The Mindset Shift: From Creator to Curator

The most sustainable visibility systems shift from creating everything to curating strategically.

➔ You're not just sharing your thoughts.

➔ You're becoming the trusted guide to valuable thinking in your domain.

This means sometimes sharing others' work with your commentary.

Sometimes asking questions instead of providing answers.

Sometimes highlighting client successes instead of your own.

Curators build authority faster than creators because they're seen as connectors, not just broadcasters.

Your System Blueprint

Right now, take one page. Draw four boxes:

- **Insight Capture:** Where will you capture ideas this week? (Choose one: notes app, notebook, voice memos)
- **Content Assembly:** What one core idea will you build this week's content around?
- Distribution Plan: Where will each piece go? (LinkedIn, email, Instagram)
- **Engagement Strategy:** Who will you engage with strategically this week? (List 3 names)

That's your system for this week.

Next week, you'll improve it.

The week after, it will feel natural.

Within a month, you'll have a visibility factory humming in the background of your business, producing recognition, opportunities, and authority while you focus on what you do best.

The Truth About Systems

A system isn't a constraint.

It's freedom.

- Freedom from wondering what to post.
- Freedom from random acts of marketing.
- Freedom from visibility is a constant mental burden.
- When you systemize visibility, you make it ordinary instead of extraordinary.
- You make it reliable instead of random.
- You make it sustainable instead of exhausting.

And that's when the magic happens:

When visibility stops being something you do and starts being something you have.

Your system awaits.

The machinery is simple.

The output is inevitable.

The next chapter gives you the exact 120-day production schedule for your new visibility factory. Turn the page when you're ready to see what consistent output creates.

CHAPTER 9

The 120-Day Production Schedule

Your Day-by-Day Visibility Factory Output

There is a warehouse in Bhiwadi that makes automotive parts. I visited it once with a client who was struggling with consistency.

➔ The owner showed me something remarkable: not the machines, but the production schedule pinned to the wall.

➔ Every machine, every worker, every output was mapped for the next 120 days.

➔ Not in vague terms, but in specific deliverables: Part numbers, quantities, quality checks, shipping dates.

He said:

"People think manufacturing is about machines.

It's really about the schedule that tells the machines what to make and when."

That's when I understood:

Visibility without a schedule is like that factory without a production plan, machines running, workers busy, but no one knows what they're actually producing.

This chapter is your visibility production schedule.

Not vague advice.

Specific daily outputs for the next 120 days.

You are the factory.

This is your production plan.

Let's begin manufacturing your presence.

The Pre-Production Week: Days -7 to 0

Setting up your factory floor before production begins.

Day -7: The Factory Foundation

- Clear one physical/digital space (a notebook, a folder, an app)
- Block 90 minutes, 3x weekly in your calendar for the next 120 days (non-negotiable)
- Tell one person: "I'm committing to 120 days of visibility. Ask me about it weekly."

Day -6: The Raw Material Audit

- List your 5 strongest professional insights (things you know that others need to know)
- List 10 client questions you answer repeatedly
- List 3 industry misconceptions you regularly correct

Day -5: The Machine Setup

- Choose ONE primary platform (LinkedIn for B2B/professionals, Instagram for B2C/visual)
- Optimize your profile completely (professional photo, clear headline, compelling bio)
- Set up your content capture system (notes app, voice memos, whatever works)

Day -4: The Quality Standards

- **Define your voice:** Professional but human? Expert but approachable? Data-driven but storytelling?

- **Choose your visual style:** Consistent colors? Specific formats? Certain types of images?
- **Set your engagement standard:** Will you reply to every comment? Engage with 3 peers daily?

Day -3: The First Production Run (Practice)

- Write one paragraph about a client success (without names)
- Record a 60-second video answering a common question
- Comment on 3 industry leaders' posts with thoughtful insights

Day -2: The Systems Check

- Test your scheduling tool (if using one)
- Create your content templates (see Appendix A)
- Set up your tracking dashboard (simple spreadsheet)

Day -1: The Commitment Ceremony

- Review your why: Why these 120 days matter to your business, your clients, your legacy
- Visualize Day 120: What will be different? How will you feel? What opportunities will have come?
- Sleep well. Production begins tomorrow.

Production Phase 1: Days 1-30 - The Foundational Output

Establishing your presence rhythm and voice.

Weeks 1-2: The Daily Output Schedule

Monday (Content Creation):

- **8 AM:** Write one insight post (300-500 words) based on your raw material audit
- **12 PM:** Engage with 5 comments on others' posts in your industry

Wednesday (Content Variation):

- **8 AM:** Create a carousel/post series from Monday's insight
- **12 PM:** Share someone else's valuable content with your commentary

Friday (Engagement & Planning):

- **8 AM:** Share a personal professional lesson (win, failure, or insight)
- **12 PM:** Plan next week's content based on what resonated

Weeks 3-4: Introducing New Production Lines

- Add one weekly video (60-90 seconds answering a question)
- Start a simple newsletter (collecting that week's three posts)
- Begin tracking: Which content types get most engagement? Save? Shares?

End of Month 1 Quality Check:

- Consistent posting rhythm established
- Engagement habit formed
- Content templates working
- First inbound inquiries noted

Production Phase 2: Days 31-60 - The Specialization Output

Moving from general presence to specific authority.

The Monthly Theme System:

Each month focuses on one core theme from your expertise:

- **Month 2 Theme:** [Your strongest professional insight]
- **Example:** For a manufacturing consultant: "Operational Efficiency in Family Businesses."

Weekly Content Clusters:

- **Week 5-6:** Deep dive into the theme
- **Week 7-8:** Case studies/examples
- **Week 9-10:** Implementation frameworks
- **Week 11-12:** Future trends/predictions

New Production Machinery Added:

- One long-form article monthly (1000+ words on your theme)
- One collaboration with a peer/partner
- One "behind the scenes" content piece showing your work process

The Feedback Integration Loop:

- Note every question received in comments/DMs
- Create content answering those questions the following week
- This creates a virtuous content cycle: Share insight → Get questions → Answer questions → Build authority

Production Phase 3: Days 61-90 - The Amplification Output

Systemizing reach and impact.

The Repurposing Assembly Line:

One core piece = Multiple outputs:

- **Monday:** Long-form article
- **Tuesday:** Social media threads from article points
- **Wednesday:** Video summarizing key insights
- **Thursday:** Carousel/infographic
- **Friday:** Newsletter compilation
- **Following week:** Podcast episode talking points

The Strategic Engagement Schedule:

- **Daily:** Engage with 3 industry leaders' content
- **Weekly:** Share 2 peers' work with meaningful commentary
- **Bi-weekly:** Comment on industry publications' articles
- **Monthly:** Participate in relevant LinkedIn/industry discussions

The Opportunity Tracking System:

Create a simple tracker:

Date	Source	Type	Status	Notes
	Content piece	Speaking invite	Accepte d	From article on...
	DM inquiry	Consulting	In talks	Asked about...

Production Phase 4: Days 91-120 - The Optimization Output

Refining based on data, not guesswork.

The Data Review (Day 91):

- Which content got the most engagement? (Not just likes, saves, shares, comments)
- Which topics generated the most inquiries?
- What time/day performed best?
- What format worked for which audience?

The System Optimization (Day 92-105):

- Double down on what worked
- Experiment with one new format
- Improve templates based on learnings
- Systemize your most effective content type

The Relationship Development Schedule:

- Map your 20 most valuable engagements from past 90 days
- Create a nurturing sequence: Like → Comment → Share → Connect → Conversation
- Schedule quarterly check-ins with key connections

The Legacy Content Creation (Day 106-120):

- Produce one "signature piece" that defines your expertise
- Create one evergreen resource (guide, checklist, framework)
- Document your 120-day journey as a case study for others

The Day 121 Output: What Your Factory Has Produced

After 120 days of scheduled production, here's what you'll have manufactured:

Tangible Outputs:

- 48+ pieces of content establishing your expertise
- 360+ strategic engagements building your network
- 1-3 long-form resources demonstrating depth
- A clear content system that runs with minimal effort

Business Outcomes:

- Consistent inbound inquiries (3-5 quality leads monthly)
- Reduced sales cycles (clients coming pre-educated)
- Increased pricing power (authority justifying a premium)
- Expanded opportunity pipeline (beyond traditional channels)

Personal Transformations:

- Confidence in your visible expertise
- Clarity in your messaging
- Systemization of your visibility efforts
- A sustainable rhythm of contribution

The Most Important Production Rule

Quality over quantity.

Consistency over virality.

Value over vanity.

Your visibility factory isn't about manufacturing the most content.

It's about manufacturing the right recognition.

One thoughtful article that helps 50 ideal clients is worth more than 100 posts that entertain thousands of strangers.

Your Production Schedule Starts Now

You have two choices:

- Keep visibility as an occasional, stressful, random effort.
- Follow this 120-day production schedule and make recognition an inevitable output of your expertise.

The machinery is ready.

The schedule is clear.

The raw material (your expertise) is waiting.

Day 1 begins when you decide it does.

Your factory is ready to produce.

Your schedule is waiting to be followed.

BECOME UNFORGETTABLE

Your visibility is about to become systematic instead of sporadic.

The final chapter isn't about more production.

It's about what happens when your factory's output changes everything.

Turn the page when you're ready for the final shift.

CHAPTER 10

The Final Shift

When Your Factory's Output Changes Everything

There is a moment in every factory's life that has nothing to do with machinery.

- It's not when the first product rolls off the line.
- It's not when they hit production targets.
- It's not even when they land their biggest client.

It's the morning, and the owner walks through the gates and realizes:

This doesn't depend on me anymore.

- The systems are running.
- The team knows what to do.
- The quality is consistent.
- The output is predictable.

The factory has become an entity, something that exists, produces, and delivers whether the owner is physically present or not.

This is the moment we've been building toward through these pages.

- Not just visibility.
- Not just authority.
- But sovereignty.

The sovereignty that comes when your presence precedes you.

When your reputation works while you sleep.

When your value is recognized before you speak.

The Morning After Day 120

Imagine waking up 121 days from now.

Your phone shows:

- 3 thoughtful comments on last night's post about industry trends
- 2 DMs from potential clients who found your case study
- 1 invitation to speak at an industry event
- Several notifications that people are sharing your framework

You haven't "posted" yet today.

You haven't "done marketing."

You haven't even had your coffee.

But your visibility factory is already working.

Because you built something that outlives your daily effort.

You created a system that recognizes you whether you're actively seeking recognition or not.

This isn't fame.

This is findability becoming inevitability.

The Three Sovereignties You've Built

1. Sovereignty Over Time

You're no longer trading hours for dollars in endless client acquisition.

You're no longer starting every relationship at zero.

You're no longer justifying your existence in every meeting.

Your time is now spent on what matters most: doing exceptional work for ideal clients who already understand your value.

2. Sovereignty Over Opportunity

Opportunities no longer come to you by chance or relentless pursuit.

They come because your visible expertise makes you the obvious choice.

When a problem arises in your domain, your name surfaces.

When a project needs leadership, your reputation recommends you.

When a conversation needs expertise, your content has already contributed.

3. Sovereignty Over Legacy

Your children won't just inherit a business.

They'll inherit a reputation.

They won't just take over operations.

They'll step into a story that's already being told.

Your name will mean something in your industry.

Not just a surname on a company board.

But a standard of how things should be done.

The Real Transformation

Let me tell you about what happens after the systems are running.

It's not about more followers. It's about fewer explanations.

It's not about more content. It's about deeper conversations.

It's not about more visibility. It's about less vulnerability.

When you're visibly expert, you stop worrying about:

- Being overlooked for opportunities
- Having to discount your value
- Starting from scratch with every client
- Your next project pipeline
- Your industry relevance
- Your professional identity

That mental space, that cognitive bandwidth, is now free.

Free for innovation. For quality. For impact. For living.

Not Just Business, But Better Business

Preeti (name changed for privacy reasons) ran a design studio for eight years.

- Good work.
- Steady clients.
- Yet a constant hustle for the next project.

After implementing her visibility system, something unexpected happened.

Clients started coming with problems instead of requests.

"We need your thinking on our brand architecture."

Instead of "Can you design a logo?"

Her revenue didn't just increase. It restructured.

- Higher-value projects.
- Longer-term relationships.
- Strategic partnerships instead of transactional work.

But here's what Preeti told me that matters more than numbers:

"For the first time, my business grows while I'm working on the work, not while I'm working on getting work."

Her visibility factory didn't just bring more business.

It brought better business.

The Choice You Make Today

Right now, as you finish this book, you stand at a crossroads you've been at before.

One path leads back to what's familiar:

- Occasional efforts at visibility.
- Random acts of marketing.

- Hope-based business development.
- The exhausting cycle of proving yourself again and again.

The other path leads to what you've just built:

- A system that makes recognition reliable.
- A presence that enters rooms before you do.
- A reputation that works while you rest.
- The liberating reality of being known for what you truly offer.

The tools are in your hands.

The blueprint is in these pages.

The system is waiting to be activated.

The Most Important Realization

Visibility isn't something you add to your business.

It's something you uncover in your expertise.

You don't become a different person to be visible.

You become more consistently yourself in more places.

The authority isn't manufactured.

It's revealed through consistent contribution.

The recognition isn't chased.

It's earned through valuable presence.

Your Next Step Is Simpler Than You Think

You don't need to implement everything at once.

You don't need to become someone you're not.

You don't need to master new skills.

You simply need to begin the production schedule.

- **Day 1:** One insight shared.
- **Week 1:** A rhythm established.
- **Month 1:** A system operating.
- **120 days:** A transformation realized.

The factory is designed.

The machinery is simple.

The raw material is your existing expertise.

All that's missing is your decision to start production.

A Final Word From My Heart

I wrote this book for one reason:

- I'm tired of watching brilliant people remain invisible.
- I'm tired of seeing expertise go unrecognized.
- I'm tired of watching value get undervalued.
- I'm tired of observing dreams get limited by visibility rather than capability.

You have something the world needs.

A skill. An insight. A solution. A perspective.

But in a noisy world, silence is a sentence.

Invisibility is a constraint.

Being unknown is a ceiling on your impact.

Break that ceiling.

Not by shouting louder than everyone else.

But by showing up more consistently as who you truly are.

Not by becoming an "influencer."

But by becoming impossible to ignore for the people who need what you offer.

The Invitation

Your 120-day production schedule begins whenever you decide.

It could begin tomorrow morning with your first captured insight.

Or next Monday with your first scheduled content block.

Or right now, with a decision that enough is enough.

Whenever it begins, know this:

Somewhere, a future client is searching for exactly what you offer.

Somewhere, an opportunity is looking for exactly your expertise.

Somewhere, a conversation needs exactly your voice.

They're waiting to find you.

Build the visibility factory that makes that discovery inevitable.

Your time to be seen starts now.

Your expertise deserves to be known.

Your value demands to be recognized.

Go build what makes that certain.

With respect and belief in what you will create,

Sumit

P.S. When you take your first step, when you share that first insight, implement that first system, experience that first inbound opportunity because of your visibility, remember this moment. Remember choosing the path of sovereignty over the path of silence. And know that somewhere, I'm cheering for you.

A Personal Invitation

If something in this book felt familiar, it's because it was written for people like you.

If you're at a point where you want to talk through your story, your visibility, and what becoming unforgettable could actually look like in your life or business, I'm open to that conversation.

This isn't a pitch.

It's a discovery call.

You can write to me directly at:

sumit@iconicedge.org

Tell me a little about who you are, what you do, and what prompted you to reach out.

If it makes sense, we'll take the conversation forward.

With intention,

Sumit Kkhubchandani

WHAT'S NEXT?
YOUR IMMEDIATE ACTION PLAN & THE PATH BEYOND THE BOOK

You've just finished reading a blueprint for transformation. Now comes the most important part: building what you've designed.

Here is your exact next-step sequence:

IMMEDIATE: The First 24 Hours

1. The Single Decision (Right Now)

- Decide on your Day 1 from the 120-day schedule. Will it be tomorrow? Monday? Today?
- Block the time in your calendar now. 90 minutes, 3x/week for the next 120 days.
- Tell one person: "I'm committing to building my visible expertise starting [date]. Ask me about my progress."

2. The Foundation Exercise (30 Minutes Today)

- Open a fresh page (digital or physical)
- Complete the Visibility Blueprint from Chapter 6:
- My Visible Anchor (3 sentences)
- My Distinctive Ground (3 completions)
- The Bridge I Build (3 answers)
- This is your operating manual. Keep it visible.

3. The Platform Setup (60 Minutes Today/Tomorrow)

- Choose your ONE primary platform (LinkedIn for most B2B/professionals)
- Optimize your profile completely:
- rofessional, approachable headshot
- Headline that states your value, not your title
- "About" section that tells your story from the Foundation Exercise
- Featured section with at least one piece of proof

THIS WEEK: Launching Production

1. The First Content Cycle (90 Minutes)

- Use your Raw Material Audit (from pre-production) or capture one fresh insight
- Create your first content piece (300-500 words or 60-second video)
- Post it
- Engage with 3 industry leaders' content meaningfully

2. The System Setup (60 Minutes)

- Set up your content capture system (notes app, voice memos, etc.)
- Create your simple tracking dashboard (Google Sheets/Excel: Date | Content | Engagement | Opportunities)
- Download/create your content templates (or use Appendix templates)

3. The First Week Review (30 Minutes Friday)

- What worked? (Format, timing, topic)
- What engagement surprised you?
- What will you do differently next week?

THE FIRST 30 DAYS: Establishing Rhythm

Your Monthly Focus:

- **Consistency Over Perfection:** Show up even when it's not perfect
- **Learning Your Audience:** What resonates? What questions do they ask?
- **System Refinement:** What parts of the process feel clunky? Streamline them

Success Metrics for Month 1:

✓ Posted consistently (3x/week)

✓ Engaged daily (10 minutes minimum)

✓ Refined your messaging based on response

✓ Received first inbound inquiry (even if small)

BEYOND THE BOOK: Your Ongoing Resources

1. Your Personal Brand Dashboard

A living document where you track:

- Content performance (what topics/formats work)
- Opportunity pipeline (inbound inquiries)
- Network growth (meaningful connections)
- Business impact (revenue tied to visibility)

2. The Quarterly Review Ritual

Every 90 days, ask:

- What visibility effort brought the highest ROI?
- What new opportunity emerged because of my presence?
- What system can I improve?
- What expertise should I deepen/expand?

3. The Evolution Path

As your visibility grows, your strategy evolves:

- **Months 1-3:** Establishing presence
- **Months 4-6:** Building authority
- **Months 7-9:** Expanding influence
- **Months 10-12:** Leveraging platform

WHEN YOU GET STUCK: The Common Challenges & Solutions

Challenge 1: "I don't have time."

- **Solution:** You scheduled 4.5 hours weekly. Protect it like your most important client meeting. Start with 90 minutes if needed.

Challenge 2: "I don't know what to share."

- **Solution:** Return to your Raw Material Audit. Share one client lesson, one industry insight, one professional realization.

Challenge 3: "No one is engaging."

- **Solution:** First, ensure you're engaging with others meaningfully. Second, experiment with formats. Third, focus on value over vanity metrics.

Challenge 4: "This feels uncomfortable."

- **Solution:** Good. Growth happens outside comfort zones. Start where you're comfortable (writing vs. video, short vs. long) and expand gradually.

THE BIGGER PICTURE: Where This Leads

In 120 days, you won't just have a "personal brand." You'll have:

A Recognized Expertise

People in your industry know what you stand for and what you solve.

A Reliable Pipeline

Opportunities come to you consistently, not randomly.

A Reputational Asset

Your name carries weight in conversations you're not even in.

A Legacy Foundation

Your visibility becomes a platform that outlives any single project or client.

AND NOW, YOUR MOST CRUCIAL CHOICE

Option A: The Solo Journey

- Follow the 120-day schedule exactly as outlined
- Join the reader community (via QR in book) for support
- Track your progress diligently
- Course-correct based on your data

Option B: The Accelerated Path

- If you want guidance, consider a structured program
- If you need accountability, find a visibility partner
- If you seek mentorship, seek expert guidance

Option C: The Hybrid Approach

- Implement the 120-day plan solo for 30 days
- Evaluate your progress and challenges
- Seek specific help only where needed

A FINAL TRUTH

The most successful people who implement this aren't the ones with the most followers. They're the ones with the most consistent commitment.

They show up when they feel like it and when they don't.

They share value when it's easy and when it's hard.

They build their visibility factory one piece at a time, one day at a time. You now have:

- The philosophy (Chapters 1-5)
- The foundation (Chapter 6)
- The principle (Chapter 7)
- The system (Chapter 8)
- The schedule (Chapter 9)
- The vision (Chapter 10)

The only missing piece is your daily execution.

BEGIN

Your first post.

Your first video.

Your first step toward becoming impossible to ignore for the people who need what you offer. That begins now.

Not when you feel ready.

Not when conditions are perfect.

Not when you have more time.

Now.

Because somewhere, someone is waiting to find exactly what you offer. Build the visibility that makes that discovery certain.

Your next step is simple:

Close this book.

Open your calendar.

Block your first 90-minute visibility session.

Then begin.

I believe in what you will build.

Your expertise deserves to be seen.

Your value demands to be recognized.

Go make it visible.

Where Your Next Chapter Begins

If this book stayed with you longer than expected,

there's probably a reason.

Some journeys don't end with the last page.

They begin after it.

If you'd like to talk through your story, your work, and how visibility fits into your next chapter, you can continue the conversation here.

This page leads to a 30-minute one-to-one discovery conversation. It's something I usually offer at ₹5,999.

For readers of this book, it's open without cost.

Not as an incentive.

As an invitation.

Scan to visit my page and decide if a conversation feels right.

No pressure.

No commitment.

Just clarity.

Because becoming unforgettable isn't about being louder.

It's about being seen by the right people, for the right reasons, at the right time.

And that work,

when done honestly,

changes everything.

With Love,

Sumit Kkhubchandani